Stand As a Mighty Oak Tree

By Ina May Pummill

Isaiah 61:3b: "They will be called oaks of righteousness, a planting of the Lord for the display of His splendor."

Stand As a Mighty Oak Tree

Unless otherwise indicated, scripture quotations are taken from the Holy Bible, New International Version.

Biblion Publishing Company L.L.C.

ISBN 9780984374823

Dedication

We who sit in awe of the heavenly display of God's glory must ourselves be inspired to dream beyond the norm and depend on the lavish resources of heaven to do the unbelievable.

Boundaries fall in pleasant places. There is much for our hands to do wherever providence has placed us. Opportunities abound for those who will respond with a passion, stirred to celebrate with wonder all that the Lord has made known through His creation and His Word.

I give thanks to the Lord for all the ways He has made Himself known to me. I am thankful for each person He has placed in my life to guide and teach and encourage me to respond to the eternal desires of my heart and use the gift of creativity to make something beautiful for the exaltation of His glory.

Introduction

One cold winter day, with snow covering all the landmarks with white, we set out on a little drive to enjoy the scenery of the surrounding countryside. It was as though we had a destination of which we were unaware. We ascended steep hillside roads to emerge on a flat opening to reveal the most beautiful vista I

remembered seeing in this area. I exhaled in a gasp at the stunning beauty of this vision of wonder. I was so enthralled with the discovery that I thought it only a one time treat, and we turned around and headed home. We did not drive further to explore other roads. It seemed this was what we were to see that day. That sense of wonder thrills me to this day. A few months later my husband came home with an amazing discovery; he had talked with a local resident with land to sell. When they went to look at the land it was this special set apart place. For thirty some years we have been blessed each day to awaken to this splendor. There have been difficulties and challenges in living in this undeveloped land, but the benefits continue to be a shining light of inspiration.

Stand as a Mighty Oak Tree

A mighty oak tree stands tall and unwavering atop a commanding hill. It has weathered many storms of every possible variety. The seasons have molded the tree and strengthened its form with unique character. This is a marvelous example for us as God works through our seasons and trials, His plan and promises to fulfill.

One does not need to travel far to behold glorious images, a galleria in a constantly changing canvas travels across the heavenly expanse, brilliantly illumined for any to see who would lift their eyes beyond present circumstances. On occasion, the display comes with such grandeur and majesty one would expect it to be accompanied by an ancient blast of trumpets, a fanfare proclaiming a message from God Himself.

By its stately stance such a mature specimen proclaims the glory of God to all who will lift their eyes to see.

The ever-changing canvas of light is beautifully framed by the graceful, uplifted branches in every season.

Through Christ Jesus, God empowers His children to stand forgiven and alive in the face of great trials as winds of worldly wisdom are certain to buffet with distracting, discouraging thoughts and disparaging insults.

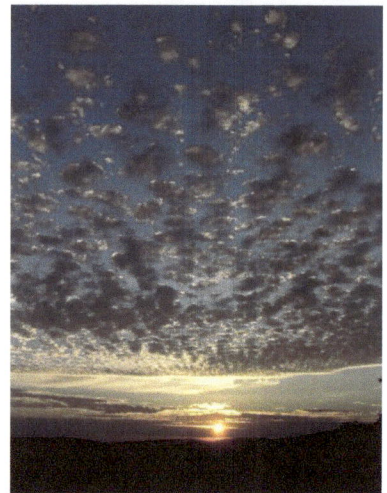

On occasion there comes a clear and glorious morning.
Clouds move eastward in dramatic departure as a rich tapestry, much like a luxurious curtain being swept aside as a magnificent prelude to begin the day. The clouds flow as waves carried along an ocean current, clearing the pathway for the azure blue heavens.
The splendor of light is woven into the pattern in exclamatory statements of joy and power.
With this sweeping symphony of light comes the refreshing melody of renewal that is spring.

Sounds of nature radiate a current of excitement in preparation for the season's awakening chorus. At every level of the atmosphere, frolicking winds toss the clouds about in colorful celebration of the morning call.
How do I respond to this glorious awakening? Do I stop and ponder with wonder at the vastness of creation? It is good to be set apart for a short while to sit in quiet stillness. It is in quietness we are enabled to reflect upon our surroundings, our challenges and trials, and to be filled with thanksgiving for the present joys that are made known to us in a myriad ways. It is in serenity that we can hear the deep things of our transformed heart to gain peace and confidence in God's leading. In this reflection streams of refreshing water overflow the soul.

This mighty oak tree is rooted in silent praise of the Creator as the changing canvas displays indescribable splendor before the eyes of my heart.
God's children are called to stand humble, steadfast and tall; blessed with words of encouragement and compassion befitting every human emotion, weeping, loving, and sharing joy while being made whole. Mere words fail to express the majestic beauty of each blossoming morning bright and bold.

The joy of light dispels darkness, especially at first light. There is something about getting up early to sit and watch for the sunrise with a fragrant cup of coffee in your hand and a camera or a notepad and pen nearby with which to record the inspiring tenor for the day. One can no more watch a sunrise passively that he could sing without a melody. The strings of the heart are tuned to respond with contagious emotions when stirred by the onset of this parade of color that precedes the ever brightening light in the fullness of day.

Ahead of each storm lies peace; Light proceeds light, to prepare witnesses for powerful display, with calm stillness going before the challenges to smooth the way.

Magnificent light rises above the storm to guide those sent to tell of the good news, revealing truth through Christ in every language while there is light of day.

Often storms come from outside the pale, beyond the place of peace and reason and respect;

Midst storms tainted by the world it is nearly impossible to discover wisdom for those who eternal truths have rejected.

Ancient words of truth go unheard or worse, mocked in turmoil stirred by hate and lies.

But we, as that oak tree, can stand in perfect peace in the face of evil tempests of any size,

Perhaps bruised and beaten, yet growing in wisdom and eternally alive.

"For the Lord Your God is with you, He is mighty to save, He will take great delight in you. He will quiet you with His love. He will rejoice over you with singing." Zephaniah 3:17

Storms often descend upon us cloaked in darkness and deceiving confusion, masked by diffused light and attended by disconcerting noise that jars the sense of wellbeing. The subtle beauty may lift our focus from present danger and allow us to miss a message of wisdom revealed by the bright light of hope that illumines our perception of the world

around us. Beyond the dark clouds of the moment, beyond the noise of distractions, shines the true light of life to remind us that we are purposed for glorious moments beyond the surrounding darkness. Many such moments are available now, even in the midst of trials. We must view all that flows from the hand of God through the lens of light. Others may intend harm through their actions; when we watch for illumined truth to shine brightly through the fearful darkness we will see God's faithfulness in unexpected brightness.

Who Am I to Wear a Cross?

Now and again there are compelling moments when the impression of the divine is as real as if I were physically stepping into the protective armor of God.

This armor is warm and loving as it enfolds me; it is strengthening and supportive for my every need but it is fierce and mighty going before me and behind me.

Such light filled moments seem almost surreal in the accompanying wonder.

In stillness, waiting and watching for direction beyond self I ponder...

Beyond worldly wisdom, beyond everything I could imagine, He is there.

Possibilities are too great for mortal man and yet the reality of such glorious thoughts strikes a chord in harmony with eternity God placed in the hearts of man.

Golden moments convict me of His deity as I walk, humbled, into a sunlit clearing.

The watching of the curling wisps of fog and the illusive light interact in the dance of the morning sunrise reminds me of an adventure in an enchanting realm.

Who am I that I might feast upon such beauty, just the Lord and me, with unity of my heart and soul transformed, at that moment transcending worldly cares and concerns?

The reality of joy is confirmed with multiple rainbows following the storm.

I am so filled with awe of the majestic presence as to fall on my knees before the creator of all such grandeur...that He would give vision to see this splendor, and ears to hear the rapturous sounds of the morning is most astonishing.

It seems at times He is waiting there in His private garden to draw me into this quiet sanctuary to be set apart, refilled with the fullness of joy that is peace in my soul.

I am humbled to have been gifted to smell the fragrance of springtime as the aromatic locust trees sing together lifting blossom laden branches heavenward in the posture of great joy. The forest seems alive with examples of His revealed glory.

This forest of hardwoods and many flowering trees is carpeted with wildflowers of soft pinks, blues and yellows mixed with the brightest of spring greens.

There is great exuberance in the very air itself as the Spirit within my heart seems to stir, keeping time with the music my ears cannot hear, the beautiful melody of the unfolding of His lavish display. There are times when I feel unworthy to wear a cross, for only through His grace has my faith been made alive to walk forgiven and to know Him upon Whom all things depend. There is always an element of surprise when a cardinal softly lands on a nearby branch to sit and sing and survey things around him. It is breathtaking when he sits with dignity displaying a regal air. He sings one of the most melodious of songs repeatedly, as if pleased with the day.

Occasional rainbows proclaim God's promise of protection of the light-clad remnant. With His covenant of the rainbow; God lavishly blesses and establishes those who are sent to plant and to water as they display the special light of love from above. In our own stormy days let us watch for the rainbows appearing in myriads of ways; they might appear as apt words of wisdom and encouragement; they may be delivered in a welcomed phone call or a letter of good news offering hope and inspiration.

The gifts of smiles and hugs may convey a sense of infinite worth to one who may have been doubting having purpose in this life.

These rays of light shine through tears of sorrow and serve to change all the tears into rainbows of hope for those who look beyond self to search the higher things of God and find healing refreshment and restoration.

It takes time. It takes perseverance. We know that there will be a day when will awaken to discover such peace as in difficult times seems impossible.

This mighty oak has been strengthened through storms and battering winds.
Fruit bearing acorns are scattered abroad in a timeless race. As we respond to storms of life, our response in words and deeds is written on the scroll of remembrance and imaged in those who stand in witness.
The light of such a faithful, trusting offering remains to the glory of God for eternity.
We are given an abundance of beautiful light with which to express our thanksgiving and humble adoration to the giver of all of life. Everything is available to respond to His commands to remember, to tell, to write of these things that reveal the faithfulness of God and that are useful to encourage, build up and edify others who delight in the God of the Bible.

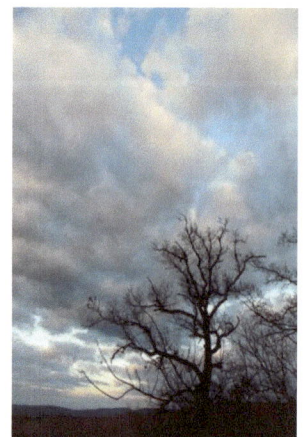

The mighty oak has grown tall through its time, protected through storms of utmost fury while other trees lie broken and torn but alive. Surviving that brokenness strengthens the tree with unique form as it continues to provide shade and beauty in every season. In God's timing, according to His plan, particular broken and bent branches will be lifted up, resurrected into fullness of abundant life to thrive.

Abundance transcends worldly comprehension, stretching the constraints of time to live victoriously in the fullness of His grace.
Ethereal moments allow an otherworldly vision of the mystery and goodness of the Lord now in this life in the stillness of this place.

Vision Transformed

Midpoint between the valley and the realm of glorious light
Along the winding river course, mingling with the low hanging clouds
Mischievous fog swirls in curious delight
Leaping with joyful abandon, carried along in harmony
With the ageless melody of time
Combining with an inclined cloud to form as a snow capped peak
Majestic in poetic beauty to thrill a peaceful soul
Perhaps a glimpse of promised splendor too lavish to extol
Yet for a moment, there is a hint of that realm beyond knowing
Real to the imagination
Entranced, watching in stillness as illusive fog keeps flowing
In a moment in time, a blink of the eye
The fog vanishes, revealing an azure sky
Memory of such a witness lives on to surface at another time
Protected in a willing heart without need or wondering to ask why.

The foggy mist glows eerily in the golden light of a new dawning. Time steps backward to another era in this ongoing history of man from his creation to the present, allowing connection to all of history. One might envision the Spirit hovering over the face of the deep now, just as at the time of the beginning.

There are those moments precious and rare when my balcony view provides a fleeting view of another time and place, when the fog rises to meet a low cloud bank giving the impression of a snowcapped mountain from my memory's storehouse. The fog is illusive and timeless in its moving about. Surely my boundaries escape earthly ties.

19

To be set apart and anointed with purpose provides rich meaning to our days, each morning is new.
We rest, not from weariness, but because our soul finds peace through trusting in the Lord with a heavenly elevated view. From such height we are given sight of the vastness of eternal certainty in every condition or swirling stormy attack.

The dawning is a process, not an instant happening. One image does not begin to reveal the height, depth, width and length of the wondrous love of God. One must sit in stillness to witness the infinate artistry of the Master as the heavens display sweeping strokes of color riding on unseen winds, ordered by the One whose breath spoke all things into being. There are dawns that arise with regal majesty, robed in shades of purple splendor, proclaiming the diety of our rightous and holy God. When we think of the journey of life with all of the little side roads of discovery it becomes evident that life is also a process of growing, maturing, and discovering the fullness of abundant life of which scripture so eloquently speaks. These visions of such lovely scenes stir the emotions to inspire creativity within us. In some perhaps it brings life to that eternal longing for more of what is good and true and beautiful. In others it impassions the creative mind to take of what has been richly given and discover the fulfillment found in working with the hands to give birth to something of beauty to make available to others. One thing is certain, that time expended quietly acknowledging with awe the display of splendor soothes the soul with the harmony found flowing through all of nature. And we have tasted something of heaven's glory as all is well with the soul.

Every morning, each season of life, is new in light of understanding upon each awakening,
When we open the eyes of the heart and stand on tiptoe, poised with eagerness to see while expectantly waiting.
As the mighty oak, let us with all of creation proclaim the glory of God in the dawning light.
We were created in His image and inspired to respond with songs overflowing heart delight.

Psalm 5:3 "Listen to my cry for help, my King and my God, for to you I pray. In the morning O Lord, You hear my voice; in the morning I lay my requests before you and wait in expectation."

The heavens, at times, appear to mirror the flowing rhythm of earthly displays of powerful splendor; in fact perhaps the opposite is true. Perhaps we recognize the melody of time in the flowing rivers, or the relentless action of the ocean waves, or the graceful branches of an oak tree precisely because we have delighted in the same harmony of movement in all of creation, most evident in the heavenly realm. One particular morning the dawn arrived with such a swift advance and powerful intensity as if it were a prairie fire sweeping across the tall grass plains. It also could easily be likened to a marvelous sunset being reflected on a great sea. It seems that often the seasons of life arrive in such a manner.

Through the dark storms of life the emerging light accompanies breaking of the clouds to allow the sunlit rays of hope assured to stream forth as if in joyful, triumphant song.

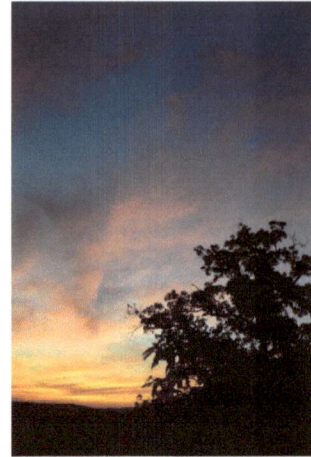

Psalm 104:2-3 "He wraps Himself in light as with a garment. He stretches out the heavens like a tent and lays the beams of His upper chambers on their waters. He makes the clouds His chariot and rides on the wings of the wind."

With the wisdom of God we are given courage to watch the majestic drama of each storm in anticipation of being strengthened and matured. Through trusting in the Lord these storms may be confidently endured. Through seeing the faithful loving kindness of God in other times of need, we are able to watch to see Him working, confident to proceed.

Foreboding clouds bring a sense of unrest, possibly of chastening or of judgment for failure to turn back to the Lord. Perhaps we lack confidence in the almighty power and glory of God. A measure of testing reveals the areas where we need strength to stand and persevere. We, as branches of the vine, are strengthened by storms to be more resilient and purposeful in responding with faith, resulting in a more vibrant personal relationship with our Heavenly Father. Always pray for His continuing work in us that draws us closer into His loving arms, that our walk will become more assured and steady.

When difficulties appear on the horizon they are very real as they threaten the calm order of our comfortable routine; we grow to depend upon surroundings as the preferred way of doing things. We must put them into perspective by measuring all things against everything we know to be true of God, and then depend upon His mercy and grace to enable us to withstand any emotional or physical battle.

As our faith is strengthened and we grow in trusting the Lord, we find solace through knowing we are not alone in any particular struggle. As we entrust our deepest concerns to those whom the Lord brings alongside to comfort us, together we may weep in view of the sufferings and rejoice in the appearance of light. The storm clouds begin to move by and we await with sure and certain hope the special blessing of perseverance where the rain and sunshine meet with resurrection power.

After the storm the representation of God's faithfulness to His promises is sweet. There is a gentle assurance revealed that brings comforting peace in remembering His loving kindness, generously displayed to those who seek His forgiveness and who sincerely desire a life changed to be aligned with His will. The oak tree can change nothing. It must stand silently and wait for the promised deliverance of all creation. By its example I am reminded that we have been given much with which to stand and make way for others to see the magnificent light of hope shining from above the wonder.

Psalm 8:1-4, 9 "O Lord, our Lord, how majestic is your name in all the earth! You have set your glory above the heavens. From the lips of children and infants you have ordained praise because of your enemies, to silence the foe and the avenger. When I consider your heavens, the work of your fingers, the moon and stars which you have set in place, what is man that you are mindful of him, the son of man that you care for him? How majestic is your name over all the earth!"

After being inundated by storms beyond our control, the light of hope reappearing to our awareness brings a progression of peace leading into rebirth of joy to resurrect a troubled soul. With the light shining through the darkness of sorrowful grief or fear we perceive that consoling reminder that our Comforter is forever near. Each occasion when we respond to this uplifting light strengthens our connection with the source of all light; we are fortified to stand steadfast as this mighty oak tree through every coming dark night. For those who have tasted the goodness of this heavenly light there is no darkness beyond its powerful reach and might.

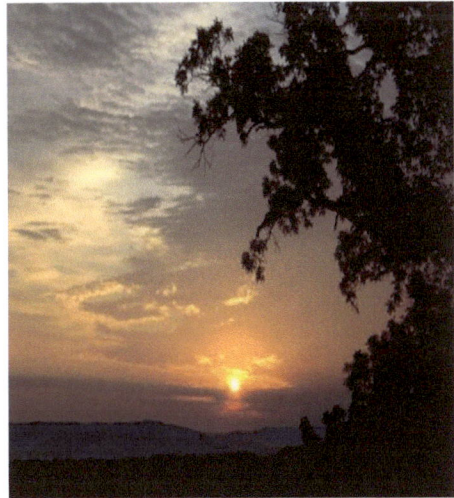

Through the many moods of light our mind and our emotions respond with every portion of our being; this oak tree is as a symbolic anchor, deeply rooted in the limestone hillside and perhaps watered by underground springs as in times of old before the rains began. In embracing such splendor as a gift of unquestionable hope from above, we must confidently respond with awe and thanksgiving for this faithful outpouring of heavenly love. That we have been given eyes to behold such grandeur with growing gratitude is another true miracle of grace from our Creator Who desires that we know Him.

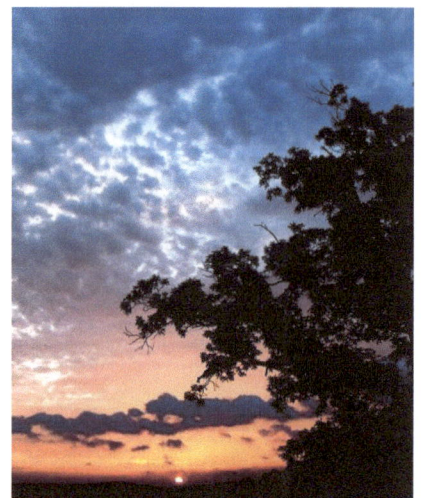

This taste of serenity and magnificence of the glory of God arouses our eternal hunger for the glorious perfection that is ever before us. Day after day we have opportunity to feast upon food that surpasses anything we might imagine or desire. In such feasting the storehouse of the heart is filled to overflowing with grace and mercy enough to pour lavishly upon others that they might also find a higher hope in the deeper truths of God.

Upon Awakening

Before the dawn began appearing on the horizon
The light of day was shining into my awaiting soul
True in the ancient sense as well as in new each morning
Waiting, anticipating the light of day I pray
Recognizing, adoring, worshiping with great thanksgiving
My Lord, my Savior Who is The Way
Set apart in stillness before going forth to meet the dawn
Before the birds begin their singing
Into the majesty of His presence I am drawn
I know His commands and His promises
I know His faithfulness through His history with man
Whatever the morning brings I await as from His hand
There will be faith strengthening lessons according to His plan
When I fail to trust Him, or grumble and complain, He is grieved
When I seek my own way through the emotion of desire
He will not go before me or afford relief
And so I ask of Him, before I choose to open my eyes
Lord, help me respond to challenge as opportunity
To bring light of truth to a dark world
Where words are merely smoke and mirrors, intended to mislead
Lord, give me grace and wisdom as a shepherd of your sheep
Inspire thoughts that will lift others toward your keep
As the faint orange glimmer of dawn makes itself known
The forest around me awakens with joyful singing
And God is revered with awe as He sits upon his throne.

Exciting Light fills those given eyes to see it with awe and wonder followed by thanksgiving for the wisdom that accompanies this supernatural light. The righteousness of God shines through the darkness in powerful display of His unending power and glory. From Isaiah 6:3 we are reminded that "Holy, holy, holy is the Lord Almighty; the whole earth is full of His glory."

Shining through the threatening clouds of this world, the exuberant light returns to awaken the melody of joy in our souls. As the song birds begin to work and sing again as the storm ceases, so too do our spirits soar when the storms of life have finished delivering their messages, making way for the refreshing light of expectation for another day.

Light so commands our attention that at times we are stopped, awestruck, by the powerful display where light pierces light to paint bright upon brighter patterns of startling impact. When the splendor of His glory reaches into the deep canyons of our times of difficult pain and grief, we are strengthened to persevere, one trusting step at a time. There is no darkness beyond the reach of the Father for those who seek the Lord.

Psalm 18:12-13 "Out of the brightness of His presence clouds advanced, with hailstones and bolts of lightning. The Lord thundered from the heavens, the voice of the Most High resounded." Psalm 68:32-33 "Sing to God, O kingdoms of the earth, sing praise to the Lord, to him who rides the ancient skies above, who thunders with mighty voice. Proclaim the power of God whose power is in the skies. You are awesome, O God, in your sanctuary; the God of Israel gives power and strength to his people."

The fog still moves upon unseen currents, fluidly, rhythmically, as if responding to ancient melodies. In this set apart place there is welcoming stillness, not lack of sound. Rather, there is an awareness of another realm blessed with absence of discord and strife; one with no tumbling or tossing of restless waves. There is patient, watchful waiting and

listening. Expectant anticipation keeps me on tiptoe to witness this flowing scene. All of nature is drawn into this visual chorus... appearing, fading from focus, and then reappearing in an otherworldly ballet. Yet it is only the movement of the fog creating this beautiful illusion. With restorative harmony in the soul one is refreshed with peace not possible in the restless clanging of the world. Throughout this display the gnarled oak tree continues to stand witness with me.

35

Through nature, God provides a healing balm as fog and mist change our perception of what is presently physically real. The essence of peace calms the soul and brings unity of heart and mind. We must be inspired to align our awareness of the unique nature of the vast power being displayed to the power that is available to lift us from ourselves into the infinite possibilities of each new day. The connection is made when in thanksgiving we stop in stillness and pray with faith in Christ.

The heavenly expanse is a vast book that displays much about God. Through His creation He has made it very plain to those who stand in witness of the swiftly changing formations, illumined by sunrises, bolts of lightning and punctuated with thunder and all the sounds of nature. God shows His love in ways beyond counting. That He is God and we are not is visible in every realm of our existence in this present life. His glory sustains all He has created.

To hear the wisdom of the ages we must be set apart in a silent place to listen quietly for the eternal melody of love through the Father's pleasure and purpose.

Mark 6:30-31 "The apostles gathered around Jesus and reported to Him all they had done and taught." Then because so many people were coming and going that they did not even have a chance to eat, Jesus told them, "come away with me by yourselves to a quiet place and get some rest." They crossed the lovely Galilee to sit upon the hillside with a calming, inspiring view. Here, on this hillside, often there is a sea of fog illumined by the pastel light of morning, perfectly prepared for repose. It seems that many times, rest is not the absence of activity or total immobility, but rather a state of mind that refuses to allow the noise of the world to divide our hearts and minds with worldly confusion. Each of us needs periods of time to be set apart in tranquility to hear with clear concentration that provides discernment and direction so that we may abide in closer relationship with all that the Lord has made possible by His redeeming work. The chains that would entangle and blind us are loosed to fall away and give freedom to walk in supernatural peace that outshines our understanding.

Seasons in life transform perception of all of life that falls within our present boundaries. We cannot control these seasons even if we desired to do so; it is a good and perfect plan that we are not gifted to interfere with the grand design of the Creator. If we were to be in control of every circumstance nothing of value would be achieved because man cannot agree with man apart from the Higher Authority. These changing seasons produce an ordering of life to bring confirming witness to the wisdom that transcends mortal minds. Man, on his own, is unable to bring order out of the chaos he creates.

Let us consider, if it were not for the ordering of the seasons we would be limited to just one color palette, one general temperature range, and the days might be all the same length and purpose. But God, in His infinite grace has blessed us with four different seasons to shine forth in magnificent, majestic splendor; each follows its life pattern for a given number of days before moving forward to make way for its new display. Nothing is left to chance in the working of God for His glory.

Spring arrives with a gentle melody, full of hope and anticipation.

This season of life comes in soft pastel hues that bathe one in calming tranquility as with a soft rain shower to bring forth new growth in that which has been sown.

If we observe the day by day blossoming into the fullness of life we are encouraged by the witness of all nature's orderly progression perfectly displaying and confirming the promises of the Lord.

With the spring comes something akin to the new birth we experience in Christ that brings exciting purpose through eternal assurance made known through the Word of God. The light yellowish green buds on the trees frame the view with the sweet hope of what is yet to be/

The redbud and other blossoming flowers of spring sing along with the returning songbirds, the whole bursting into melodic praise for another season of grace in which to rejoice.

The appearance of spring comes softly at first, perhaps as a prelude to the wonders of eternity being measured out in lavish gifting until that glorious day when we will see the fullness of splendor completely outshining the things of earth.

This is true abundance present boundaries cannot contain; overflowing riches streaming through seemingly simple things lavished with eternal purpose, born before time began. Once begun, spring awakening bursts forth with gladness after the restful slumber of winter solitude. It renews our hope and revives our expectant joyful attitude.

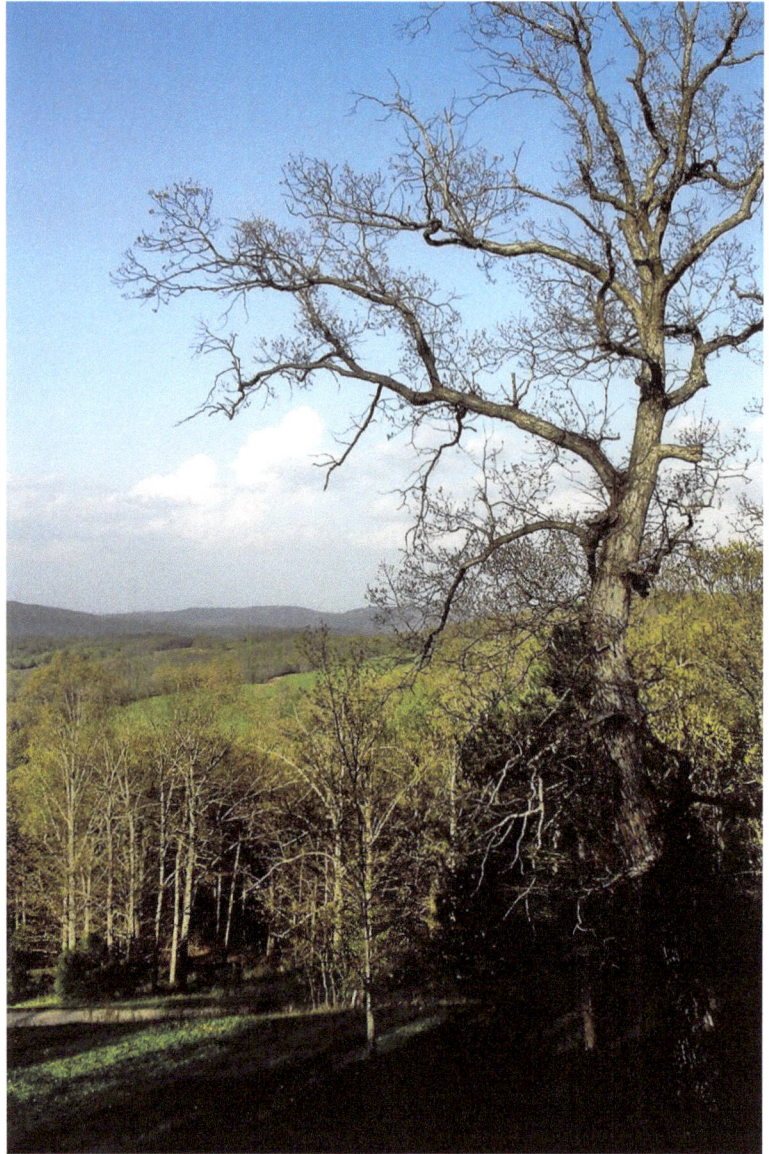

All things are new when we welcome each day with a higher view of God. We are energized to begin cleaning, building, reaching out to others to renew friendships and reflect upon the many ways a person or an incident or occasion has had influence in the direction of our lives. The relationships we have been given with friends, family and unlikely people become part of the tapestry of life that heightens our awareness of the blessed abundance of this time of preparation for all eternity. It is the quality of such relationships based upon thoughts, ideas and shared experiences that make possible unbreakable bonds uniting us even when the time of influence may be short. The heart is a vast storehouse for both lifetime memories and for the precious words of scripture to reside, to guide and to inspire the wise use of the time we have been given.

There is something of a particular nature in this tranquil early summer sunrise. A bit of fog hangs low in the valley and the sun appears red as it rises above the distant mountain. It seems all this is happening near the horizon while the rest of the sky overhead is still tinged with the steel blue color of the night. The color is so flamboyant that it disrupts the solitude and peacefulness of the moment to color the coming day with great excitement. I have heard older relatives speak of burning daylight. In earlier times it was considered laziness to be lying about sleeping when there was much work to be done. It is easy to see how the vibrancy of such a display of light would instill a desire to be quickly about the business of the day. Especially, since we cannot be certain what tomorrow will bring, we must actively await its coming by making the most of each opportunity and each possibility that accompanies this day. This is the day in which we are able to respond in a timely manner to all the small things that may influence the lives of others to desire that same fullness of abundant life in Christ for their own fulfillment. It is when our life is most closely aligned with God's will that we find contentment and satisfaction accompanying every step of this journey for the time allotted. This brings glory to God.

Fullness of summer comes about with a sharp contrast to the misty spring mornings. Just days before this the mornings were soft and tinted with pastel shades; the eastern sky is now surrounded with crisp colors of the swiftly arriving sunrise. Where there had been sweet scents of the flowering locust trees now there is a more earthy fragrance as the summer growing season is well established. It is a time of order and routine. It is a time of contentment even in the discontentment of daily challenges and disruptions. The ordering of the process of life is a stable foundation for responding to the unexpected.

Summer abundance is the fruit of spring planting and giving of self to nourish and encourage growth through enabling the emerging gifts of others to bear fruit that will last. Nehemiah 9:12 "By day you led them with a pillar of cloud and by night with a pillar of fire to give them light on the way they were to take." There is nothing quite like sitting outdoors on a humid summer afternoon in witness of such a magnificent cloud billowing upward in rapid expansion, then flattening as it reaches a different layer of the atmosphere. Often, it seems, we experience periods of life when the pieces of the puzzles in our lives come together in subtle understanding. For a while we find the exciting growth in understanding flowing into an awareness of purpose pouring through the works of our hands. When more of the fullness of unity of the effort begins to overflow it may spread around the world, where ever the winds of providence may carry it according to a preordained determination beyond understanding.

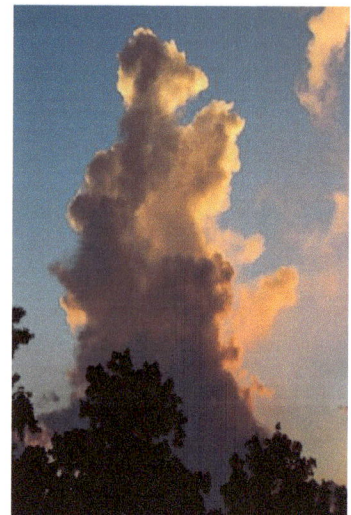

Later on, established in the lush growing season of summer, there are frequent dramatic cloudbursts that swell to an intense downpour over a small area, seemingly almost instantaneously sending gushing streams for a short time. Frequently these may be accompanied by a brilliant rainbow as in celebration of much needed blessing. A swiftly flowing breeze may lower the temperature and provide a time of relief. We might be facing a storm of life that seems unbearable. To pause in wonder of this cooling rain shower can lift our minds from that which troubles us and at the same time may bring healing to the trials we are facing. To sit with face upturned to welcome the sweet raindrops and allow the cooling breeze to lift awareness above present trials brings peace that reminds believers that all is well with our souls when our hope is in the Lord.

Fading Breath of Summer

Amidst delight and exuberance
A longing for an essence
noticeably out of reach
Summer is a time of tilling the soil,
sowing, reaping, giving out
A hunger for that quiet path of
restoration to be refilled
Along the way there appears a bit
of mountain crispness
Astonishment accompanies a gasp
of breath in the chill
A lingering summer tanager
sounds a cry without answer
The cacophony of strife stills as
Hummingbirds begin their arduous journey
Glossy leaves on black gum trees sing in
magnificent red
They loosen their grasp, drifting in
downward circles
Carried along on a wisp of wind
To lie along a dusty roadside gleaming in
the grass
The late afternoon sun shines through tall trees
To illumine the leaves with special light
Shorter days allow time for pondering and awaiting insight
For hearing what the Spirit brings to mind
To refresh and refill the storehouse of the heart
There is an abundant harvest of treasure from which to pour out love
Lengthening shadows reveal a dramatic landscape
Golden leaves glow with more vibrancy in the evening sun
And tendrils of fog lift upward in the cool as the day is done
In a special way my soul is in tune with the seasons
I am compelled to praise God for many reasons
Autumn takes its cue, painting the landscape with every hue
How marvelous the surrounding forest of rust and gold
Like the color of the pavement in Jerusalem of old
Oh to stop and allow that warmth to envelope my soul
My whole being rejoices in the process of being made whole
As a spectator of the changing of the guard
One season hands the baton to the next
It gives witness to the faithfulness of the creator
Just like promises, each season arrives in designated time
Though we may not recognize its presence apart from changing leaves
Warming or cooling temperatures or migrating birds and butterflies
The soul may sing out at hearing the cries of wild geese over head
Cold winds may come early and we walk in brisk exhilaration

Like a child, we may watch for exhaled breath to stream forward in frozen display
Golden rod smiles with warmth enough to store in memory
To chase the cold with reflections of a time of blossoming
Perhaps that warmth is felt when sitting beside a fireplace watching the brightly colored flames, wrapped in an afghan while allowing the mind to search for memories. Colors reach their brightest intensity before falling away into the changes that are coming. The storehouse grows richer with the wealth of memories as time moves forward. How is it that the aging process brings about these same types of displays as our personalities blossom while the bodies begin to take on the pastel aura of growing wisdom and contentment that accompanies greying hair and slower steps? Beauty shines with a patina brought about through the lessons of life, much as when a treasured pearl imparts an opaque richness as the light seems to penetrate more deeply into its lustrous skin.

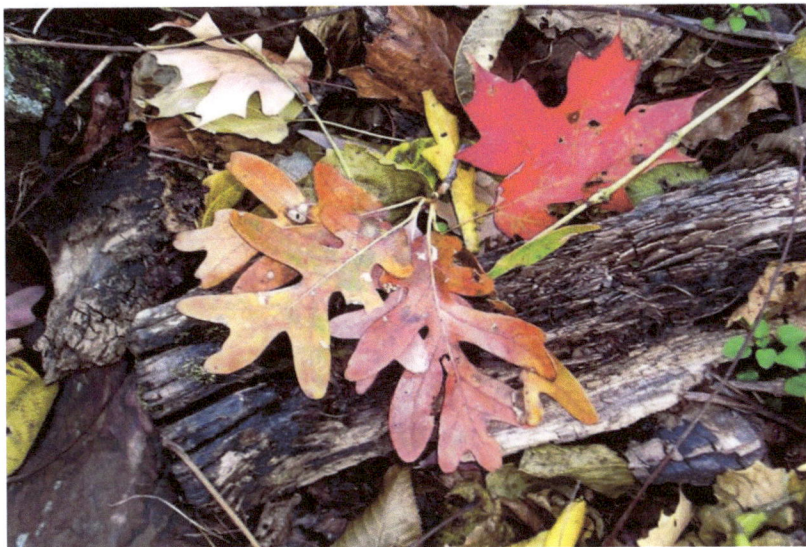

Autumn is a time of celebration; a time of reward and satisfaction as seen in the golden light of triumphant living, even in the face of challenge and suffering as we are carried along by the Spirit. The richness shines as jewels in late afternoon light and we delight in such earthly beauty that will fade much too soon. We may be blessed with a feeling of contentment and satisfaction as we learn to rest in the Lord's enabling.

Autumn might be viewed as a kind of a kaleidoscope through which all of the fruiting harvest is brought together as brilliant jewels into a complex pattern of exciting designs that display the abundance of the season. As the mighty oak tree itself is transformed into golden beauty before entering another season of rest, we too might be surprised to witness the tapestry of each life, to see the pattern of light being revealed through brokenness to selfish ways. To persevere is often difficult and challenging but the rewards are amazing. Each autumn brings celebratory understanding of present glory in relationship to the not yet fullness of expression of being created in the image of God. Winter will follow with set apart time to ponder and rest in preparation for another season of growing and bearing of fruit that will last. Meanwhile, the forest floor is carpeted with colorful leaves of different species of oaks and maples displaying all of the colors of autumn.

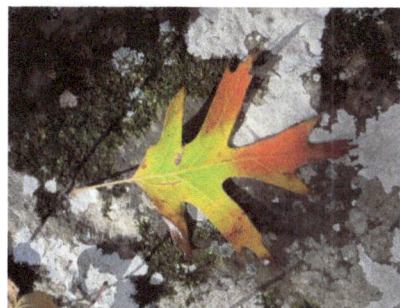

In Perfect Stillness

Softly, gently, quietly drift downward perfectly formed crystals of snow
Each unlike the other and yet the same....God's endless creativity blessing us with beauty
With the snowflakes falling for hours in the stillness of His presence,
Covering the broken, the ugly, the plain...Covering the beautiful just the same;
The snow softly covers traces of man's imperfections
At the same time outlining and making God's creations appear even lovelier.
Graceful tree branches, red berries, the contrast of evergreen cedars and leafless oaks
reaching upward to the sky,

The contours of the hills and meadows are made more distinct by the snow.
The birds cease their singing; the deer stay quietly in their woodland shelter.
It is a time to reflect on God's tender mercies.
My footsteps break the pristine perfectness of this soft white carpet.
I walk peacefully through this serene earthly cathedral,
Nothing compares with God's paintings; His canvas is perfection in form and light. Even
the soft, subdued light of a wintry morning cannot be duplicated in any medium.
I turn my face upward and snowflakes brush my cheeks. I feel the fullness of the silence. As
I stand quietly, expectantly, I feel His encompassing authority in the form of gentle love.
It is a time of reverent and humble thanksgiving.
Peace rides on the gentle breeze of tranquility as a soothing melody of love.
He has refreshed and restored me in perfect stillness.

It is in the stillness of winter, perhaps transformed under a layer of sparkling snow and ice, that we find peace and a sense of stillness through the gift of resting in the ONE Who is sovereign over every manner of providence. This oak tree has no defense against the harsh realities of being laden with the heavy ice. How fortunate are we to be blessed with warm homes and windows through which we may behold such harsh beauty. In the early morning light the scene is almost ablaze with golden diamonds dazzling in united perfect harmony for this season in time. We too should appear united in such light.

Growing maturity in wisdom and understanding brings improved hearing. According to the prophet Isaiah in 30:21, whether we turn to the right or to the left we are to stop and listen for direction. In turning to the right one icy morning I was strengthened by confirmation of a particular way I was to go, with understanding through the firmament's display. The swiftly moving clouds formed as the wings of eagles and the light appeared as a dove. Isaiah 40:31, John 1:32 This was a reminder of His promise to carry me as on eagles wings and that His light would not forsake me.

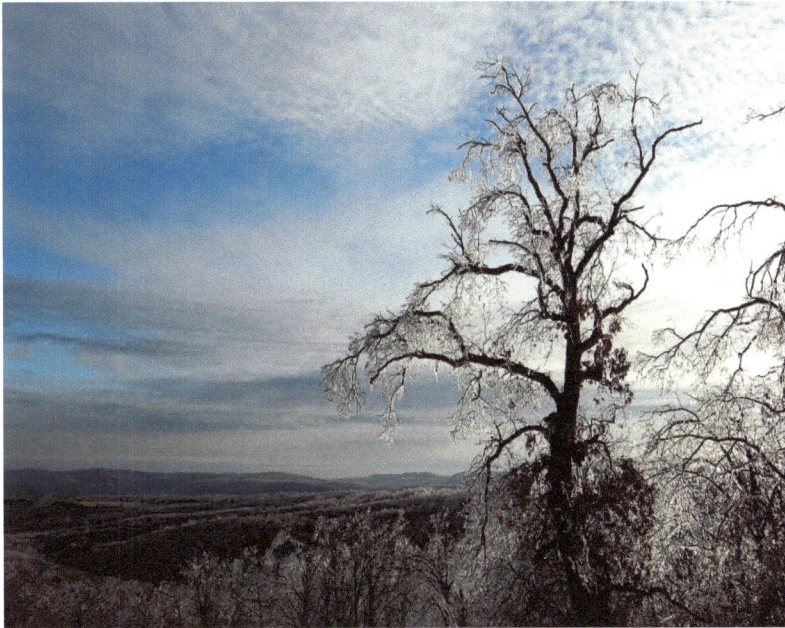

Often the aftermath of any storm leaves trials to further strengthen us to endure the race. Winter challenges, though beautiful, leave no doubt that we are not in charge of time or place. In all things may we watch for the light of understanding and be given sight to witness unique beauty even when it does not fit our comfort or our desires. Even in the discomfort in dealing with winter storms or in relationships, let us look beyond present stumbling blocks and watch for the amazing grace of patience, wisdom and even submission. We may discover sweet treasure among the thorns that seek to distract us and rob us of our peace.

This display of heavenly glory and magnificent power brings to mind this wisdom from the book of Romans in chapter one, verse 20: "For since the creation of the world God's invisible qualities-His eternal power and divine nature- have been clearly seen, being understood from what has been made, so that men are without excuse." How could one stand beneath this towering illustration of wrath and judgment that await those who are not mindful of His commands? Almost like the parting of the Red Sea waters, this awesome spectacle of unlimited power should humble us to fall to our knees in reverence toward God, the Creator of everything that exists. To behold such evidence of God's authority even over the clouds of the air must confirm the magnificence of our Heavenly Father. Even the winds and waves obey the Mighty One.

There is a majestic hymn that comes to mind, written by Isaac Watts in 1719 that comes to mind in word and triumphant melody each time I see something such as this photograph displays. "I Sing the Almighty Power of God" in all its verses celebrates God in the fullness of His splendor and infinite power in relationship to the magnificence of His creation.

In Isaiah chapter 6 Isaiah writes of the vision of the Lord seated on a throne, high and exalted, and with the train of His robe filling the temple. The seraphs were calling to one another: "Holy, holy, holy is the Lord Almighty; the whole earth is full of His glory." Isaiah responded crying "Woe to me...my eyes have seen the King, the Lord Almighty!" Do we respond with that same awe when we behold a glimpse of the glory of God? He is not silent. We sing because we cannot remain silent.

The firmament is a vast canvas upon which God displays a rich abundance of life and vision. It is constantly changing, accompanied with flashes of lightning, a symphony of wind and thunder and soft sounds of raindrops falling, all in the harmony and rhythm of the light flowing as an eternal river. Often the images are as impressionistic exhibitions of a realm just out of reach, a promise of the splendor that awaits those who wait upon the Lord with all their mind, heart and soul. We cannot begin to grasp the incomprehensible infinity that awaits our discovery for all the days of eternity.

Psalm 108:4-5 "For great is your love, higher than the heavens; your faithfulness reaches to the skies. Be exalted, O God, above the heavens, and let your glory be over all the earth."

In the early dawn as in the fading light of day the bright beams still reach for a moment to wash the heavens with bright colors. Surely the clouds sing the praise of their creator as the light gives other worldly shapes and textures to the silent forms. It seems at times that surely the clouds are tongues of fire with messages of repentance leading to renewed hope and direction.

The Beauty of Each Storm

From the stillness of the afternoon a slight ripple of air touches my face
A coolness as the breeze changes pace, I sense freshness...a lightness of feeling
The breeze turns to intermittent gusts
Turning to look into the strengthening wind
I see a line of storm clouds pushing and climbing higher
Lightning bolts streak across the sky as many fingers of energy at the same instant
Lower levels of clouds are swirling in different directions
The white line of the rain moves steadily up the valley
God, this is an awe-inspiring illustration of Your magnificent power!
I sit in silence, captivated by this example of Your creation
The rain is upon me; the coldness of the drops is refreshing
There is not a sound but for the melody of the rain
It is a soothing comforting sound which erases cares of the day
As suddenly as the storm came, the torrents cease
The darkness parts as an intense burst of sunlight pierces the scene
Showers of fine mist play in the sunshine
A beautiful rainbow arcs across the valley to the hills beyond
Another of Your miracles, God! You are infinite in Your creation.
Each storm in nature shows Your unlimited creativity.
So too, are each storm and each rainbow different in my life.
The storm passes, leaving the life sustaining gift of water
Though the rainbow is fleeting, it too reminds me of Your promises
It remains a vision in my mind which I can recall at will.
Oh how You care for your people Lord!
Oh how You keep giving us reminders of Your faithfulness and love.
As the clouds begin to move past, the birds begin their singing
They go about their duties refreshed and busy with their simple life
I sit a bit longer, transported to another realm of thinking
As I search the scene before me for every detail You put in place
Then the sun sinks low toward the horizon
The remaining clouds begin to reflect the brilliant colors of evening
Only You could have imagined and created such splendor
The clouds are moving, the light is ever changing
You, Lord, are to be praised for Your unceasing gifts of beauty
Thank You for giving me eyes with which to see the beauty of each storm.

With a final flourish the golden light touches the clouds to leave lasting impressions of the grandeur and almighty power of God as peaceful preparation for rest, trusting in His presence to carry us through the night time hours.

And the mighty oak tree stands silently in witness of it all.
Isaiah 65:22b "For as the days of a tree, so will be the days of my people; my chosen ones will long enjoy the works of their hands."

Evening Communion

Evening is a special time for thought
The activities of the day are slowly set
aside. The sun steadily moves lower on
the horizon...
Golden light touches the tips of the
trees with lingering grace.
Beautiful colors fill the heavens with
increasing saturation and every
cloud is brushed with special soft
warm golden glow. God surely chose
colors to remind us of the richness of
His lavish love! This divine love calms and comforts us as we pause to rest in Him.
This love magnifies the beauty we see when we take time to look deeply... though we see
imperfectly now, understanding is illumined by the ancient light.
A slight haze gently softens the landscape as the shadows lengthen and there is a slight
movement of air as the coolness moves up the mountain. Oh! How God must sing with
delight when we stop in reverence,
He must smile when we pause to savor the beauty with which He has surrounded us.
Oh! What peace He brings to our cluttered minds, if only we wait in stillness watching.
He must rejoice when we walk in His light praising Him with every thought.
Later in the evening, the quiet time is interrupted by the gentle sound of raindrops.
I close my eyes and allow the soothing rhythm of the falling rain to lull me to sleep.
God lifts our thoughts above cares and burdens in beautiful ways.
He turns our prayers toward Him in adoration and thankful worship for His blessings.
Many are the blessings He lavishly bestows upon those who respond with His light to see.
The rain falls on all, but only few pause to hear its melodious sound.
Few respond to the delightful fragrance of the refreshing showers. Few lift their arms with
abandon to twirl in delightful circles with the excitement of a child.
Very few see the rainbows in the light of God's covenant with His people.
In the nighttime hours the rainbow remains visible in the eyes of my soul, illuminated by
the light of God's eternal love in my heart...woven into the tapestry of my life.
Because God has given us the Light of the World we need never walk lost in darkness.
Each morning has a distinctive peace and grace made known through eagerly receiving
the gift of life and responding wholeheartedly to all its possibilities.
Evening communion with the Father is perfect preparation for resting through the night
in His care. Oh! Let us watch in the direction of the sun's setting. Let us delight in the
fading light for we do know that what is yet to be is not fading or fleeting, but is the
crown of present hope fulfilled. At times the golden light-tinged clouds form an opening
that seems to be a window into another realm but in reality serves to inspire the
imagination with such a glorious glimpse into the far reaches of time.
Above the fog filled valley, beyond the window of time, the higher reaches of the
firmament still shine with the dark blue as a perfect backdrop for the pink brush strokes
that highlight the scattered clouds
Perhaps a long forgotten dream might come to mind; a reflection of a moment in time
when the emotion of awe and wonder overflowed in a song of praise.
Let us confidently close our eyes in restful, restoring sleep to wait expectantly for the dawn
of another day.

Even as the light is fading in the west, we know the darkness cannot contain the light. We rest, knowing the sunrise is on its way with which to begin a new day with unknown opportunities

Let us hold tightly to these impressions of the light of God's faithfulness that enable us to persevere in this season of preparation for the glories to come to those rooted in Christ Jesus our Lord. What we recognize expressed in the heavens is a mirror of what is filling our hearts. The gift of gaining vision of the light reveals the hope of eternity singing from a heart and soul restored to discover fullness of life. Such abundance is treasure in heaven with eternal value. It is when we are most content and satisfied in the Father through the Son that He is most glorified. That contentment and joy spills over to flow as a glorious and mighty river to spread that banquet of joy to faraway places. Blessing follows blessing, always. The blessing often arrives in unexpected wrappings for which we need prayer to discern and celebrate. God alone is worthy to receive all glory forever and ever. He alone knows what it will take to refine His people as gold and He will accomplish the work He has begun. Let us be ever watchful to see glimpses of His purpose in each day, the difficult as well as those that seem a delight. Both serve to train and to nourish us to stand as this mighty oak tree for a time and a season according to His purpose from before the beginning was spoken into being. When the desires of our hearts are aligned with what we know to be true of God according to His Word He will delight in responding to our prayers in the manner that brings us the most good and crowns Him with glory. And for this, let us overflow with praise to His glorious grace forever. Amen.

Psalm 37:3-4 "Trust in the Lord and do good; dwell in the land and enjoy safe pasture. Delight yourself in the Lord and He will give you the desires of your heart."